ANIMAL PREY

Skunks

SANDRA MARKLE

⌐ LERNER PUBLICATIONS COMPANY / MINNEAPOLIS

THE ANIMAL WORLD IS FULL OF PREY.

Prey are the animals that predators eat. Predators must find, catch, kill, and eat other animals in order to survive. But prey animals aren't always easy to catch or kill. Some have eyes on the sides of their heads to let them see predators coming from all directions. Some are colored to blend in and hide. Some prey are built to run, leap, fly, or swim fast to get away. And still others sting, bite, or use chemicals to defend themselves.

Four kinds of skunks live in North and South America. They protect themselves from predators with a foul-smelling spray. *The striped skunk is the most common skunk living in the forests of North America.*

It's a warm July night in a northern Wisconsin forest. A female striped skunk pokes her head out of the hollow log where she has spent the day. After sniffing the air, she looks around for any sign that a predator is lurking nearby. Then she climbs out of the log and sets off in search of a meal, waddling slowly on her short legs. She's about the size of a chubby housecat and getting fatter by the day. The skunk doesn't go very far before she stops to nibble. First, she eats some leaves and fresh green buds. Then she pounces on a spider and eats it. A little farther on, her sharp sense of smell leads her to an earthworm underneath the leaf litter covering the forest floor. The sturdy claws of her front paws are designed for digging. She uncovers the worm and eats this juicy mouthful. Then she waddles on.

The coats of many prey animals are colored to help them blend in and hide. But a skunk's black coat has a white stripe on its back that ends in a white fringe on either side of its tail. The coloring and markings are designed to make sure other animals notice it. When they spot a skunk, most predators, such as bobcats, badgers, foxes, and coyotes, will move away. They know that skunks produce an extremely foul-smelling oily liquid that they can spray if they are threatened.

But high up in a tall tree at the edge of the forest meadow, one predator isn't bothered by the skunk's odor.

A great horned owl hears a rustling in the grass below and swivels its head toward the sound. Spotting the female striped skunk, the owl's big yellow eyes open wider. The hunter watches as the skunk follows its sharp sense of smell to a quail's nest.

Skunks are prey for owls. But for quails, skunks are predators. Seeing the skunk, the mother quail flaps her wings and flies to safety a short distance away. The female skunk digs into the quail eggs the quail mother left behind. The skunk pushes one egg away from the others with her nose. Holding this egg between her paws, she breaks open the shell with her sharp teeth. Then she laps out the gooey contents.

As evening slowly fades into night, the skunk eats two more eggs. High in the tree, the owl waits for its chance. When the skunk waddles out of the quail's nest, the hunter spreads its wings and takes flight. The owl's wing feathers are as flexible as rubbery fingers, so it can sweep through the air nearly silently. The skunk doesn't hear the approaching owl. But just in time, she sees the hunter's shadow.

The skunk doesn't use her defensive spray against this predator. With most attackers, the oily droplets of spray would cause temporary blindness. But the owl has an extra set of see-through eyelids that slip across its eyes as protective goggles. The skunk can only run away.

Skunks can run fast for short distances. The female sprints to a hollow log and squeezes inside. The owl sweeps past and soars upward again on pumping wings. From the safety of her hideout, the skunk watches the owl circle overhead. At last, the hunter flies away in search of easier prey.

When she feels safe, the female striped skunk goes in search of more to eat. This time, she visits a campground. Finding an overturned garbage can, she digs in. Skunks will eat all kinds of fruits, nuts, insects, frogs, mice, and even garbage. The female skunk isn't fussy. She munches on a wrapper and the tasty bits inside.

By the time dawn's first light filters through the forest, the female striped skunk is curled up in a hollow log. Skunks sleep most of the day and come out to search for food in the evening. As winter approaches, darkness slips into the forest earlier every day, and the air begins to get colder.

One afternoon the skunk discovers the ground is covered with cold, white snow. Snowflakes stick to the skunk's coat without melting. Her thick, downy undercoat traps body heat next to her skin, keeping her warm. That night she catches a mouse. Then standing on her hind legs, the skunk manages to reach a branch loaded with berries.

The snow keeps falling, and the forest floor is soon covered. It's not as easy for the skunk to find anything to eat. She leaves the forest to search for a meal in a nearby cornfield.

She finds a little dried corn to eat among the remains of a farmer's corn crop. Later, she also digs up some grubs. Then she discovers fallen apples on the ground and has a feast.

The snow gleams brightly as the last of the moonlight combines with the first light of day. Full and ready for her daylong nap, the female skunk waddles back toward the woods in search of a safe place to sleep. Suddenly, the sound of a young coyote makes her stop and turn around. The young coyote stops too. It's his first winter of searching for food. For a moment, predator and prey stare at each other across the snow.

When the coyote doesn't immediately leave, the female striped skunk goes on the defensive. She fluffs up her fur to make herself look as big as possible, sticks her bushy tail straight up, and stomps her front feet.

The young coyote ignores this display and comes closer. The female skunk arches her body. With both her rear end and her head aimed at the hunter, the skunk contracts muscles to tighten her rear end. Tiny nipples push out of the scent glands on either side of her anus, the opening from which she deposits wastes.

Skunks' supply of stinky oil is just enough to squirt out about five or six blasts of about one soupspoon each. After that, it will take at least a few hours to produce enough oil to fire again. Skunks can aim their spray accurately from as many as 10 feet (about 3 meters) away. The female skunk is much closer to the coyote than that. The coyote comes even closer, so the skunk finally uses her most powerful defense. The young coyote yelps as the droplets of spray strike its left eye, and it runs away from the foul scent. The skunk escapes and heads home.

Later that day, the female skunk moves into a den. She shares it with two other skunks, another female and a male. Another snowstorm piles snow over the entrance to the den. The skunks could dig themselves out, but they don't. Instead, the three skunks curl up close together and sleep through the cold winter days and nights. This way, all three skunks stay warm, living off the stored fat in their bodies. When the air warms up for a few days, the skunks dig out and go to the nearby stream for a drink. They also hunt for food. Sometimes the females catch mice. Other times, they make a meal of acorns and whatever else they can find. When heavy snows fall again, the skunks return to their den and go back to sleep.

Finally, spring arrives and the snow melts away. The female striped skunk returns to her routine of sleeping during the day and foraging (searching for food) at night. Never picky about her meals, she gnaws on an old bone she finds in the grass. Then she eats some of the tender green shoots around her. She also uses her long, sturdy claws to root through the soil, flicking out insect grubs. She gulps them down.

One evening she finds a wild turkey's nest. When the female turkey flees, the female striped skunk feasts on the eggs.

Late in March, the female striped skunk mates. One night in early May, she gives birth to five babies, called kits. At birth they're as tiny as newborn kittens. They have only a thin layer of hair, but they already have their black-and-white striped markings. Their eyes and ears are closed. All day the female skunk curls around her babies, keeping them warm and letting them nurse.

At night she leaves briefly to forage close to the den. She returns often to let her babies nurse. With frequent feedings, the kits grow quickly. By the time they're three weeks old, they're beginning to get their fur coats and their eyes and ears open. The female skunk is able to leave her kits alone for longer periods of time.

One night while the female skunk is away, a badger discovers the skunks' den. The youngsters try to defend themselves. They are already producing smelly liquid, but they can't yet spray it far. When the kits raise their tails to fire, the oily droplets only ooze out. This doesn't bother the badger. It eats two of the kits and leaves.

When she returns home, the female skunk smells the badger's lingering scent. She can tell what happened to her missing babies. Since she can't guard her litter all the time, she will move them. One at a time, she carries the remaining kits, a male and two females, in her mouth to an abandoned muskrat den. She would have moved the youngsters shortly anyway. The old den was fouled with the kits' wastes. It may have been this scent that attracted the badger.

Living in a new part of the forest, the female striped skunk can forage in a new part of her home range. She has a fresh supply of food and can return frequently to nurse and check on her growing youngsters. Bigger, stronger, and more coordinated, the month-old kits explore outside the den whenever their mother leaves them on their own.

Attracted by interesting smells, the little male goes off alone. Before he gets into any trouble, though, his mother returns. She leads him and his siblings into the den and lets them nurse. Then she curls up with her family to sleep the day away.

The young skunks continue to grow. Soon they go along with their mother on her foraging trips. By late August, they're foraging on their own. The young females stay in the area that's now familiar to them. One female is quickly caught and eaten by a great horned owl. Their brother wanders a little farther every night. Soon he's searching for food in an area that's completely new to him. And one night, he encounters something else that's new—a fox. The hunter stops in its tracks and studies the skunk.

The young male is naturally bold. He takes his defensive stance. Hissing and stomping his feet, he fluffs up to look even bigger than he is. He also lifts his bushy tail, advertising he's ready to fire his foul-smelling spray. The fox is bigger and stronger than the young male, but it remembers an earlier meeting with a skunk. The fox trots away to search for easier prey.

As another winter approaches, the young male finds a den of his own. The surviving young female rejoins her mother and moves into a den they'll share for the winter. It's a good den under a large rock, but they won't have it all to themselves. An older male soon joins them. The male settles between the females and the den's entrance. He'll fight off any other males who try to enter.

All winter, the mother and daughter huddle together with the older male. On his own, the young male heads out on warm days to search for food. He needs energy to stay warm. In the spring, he goes in search of a mate as well as food. The older female and her daughter both mate with the male they wintered with. Then each goes out to forage alone. About two months later, each female finds her own den and gives birth to a litter of babies. In a nearby area, the young male's mate gives birth too. So another generation of skunks joins the cycle of life, a constant struggle to survive between predators and prey.

Looking Back

- Take a close look at the skunk on page 33. Check out the sharp teeth that it uses to catch and kill prey of its own.

- Look again at the skunk eating the quail's eggs on page 9. Observe how the skunk uses its front paws to help it eat its meal.

- Are skunks herbivores, eating only plants? Are they carnivores, eating only other animals? Or are they omnivores, eating a variety of both plants and other animals? Look back through the photos, and make a list of all the different kinds of food you see the skunks eating.

Glossary

DEN: an animal's shelter

HOME RANGE: the area in which a skunk usually searches for food

LITTER: a group of babies born at one time

NEST: an area prepared by an animal to provide a place to raise its young

NIPPLE: a small projection from a gland. The skunk aims its spray from the nipple on its anal glands.

PREDATOR: an animal that hunts and eats other animals in order to survive

PREY: an animal that a predator catches to eat

More Information

BOOKS

Jacobs, Lee. *Skunk.* Farmington Hills, MI: Gale Group, 2002. This book is an introduction to the habits of different kinds of skunks.

Patent, Dorothy Hinshaw, and Michael Kalmenoff. *Weasels, Otters, Skunks, and Their Family.* New York: Holiday House, 1973. This book introduces the behavior and features of the various members of the weasel family, including skunks.

Whitehouse, Patricia. *Skunks.* Chicago: Heinemann Library, 2002. This book provides an introduction to a skunk's physical features, what it eats, and where it lives.

VIDEO

National Geographic Really Wild Animals: Secret Weapons and Great Escapes. National Geographic, 1997. See skunks and lots of other animals using their special weapons and abilities to escape from predators.

WEBSITES

Skunk Activities
http://www.zoobooks.com/newFrontPage/animals/virtualZoo/petskunks.htm. This site is packed with activities about skunks and their close relatives.

Striped Skunk
http://www.hww.ca/hww2.asp?pid=1&id=104&cid=8
Discover lots of facts about skunks.

Index

With love for Noah Beckdahl

The author would like to thank the following people for sharing their expertise and enthusiasm: Dr. Yeen Ten Hwang and Travis Quirk, Department of Biology, University of Saskatchewan, Canada. The author would also like to express a special thank-you to Skip Jeffery for his help and support during the creative process.

Photo Acknowledgments

The images in this book are used with the permission of: © Eileen R. Herrling/ ERH Photography, pp. 1, 35, 37; © Tom and Pat Leeson, p. 3; © D. Robert & Lorri Franz/ CORBIS, p. 4; © Maslowski Photo, pp, 7, 9, 12, 14, 17, 25; © Stephen Dalton/ Animals Animals, p. 8; © Royalty-Free/ CORBIS, p. 10; © Thomas Kitchin & Victoria Hurst, pp. 13, 31; © Jan Wassink, pp. 15, 19; © Michael Quinton, pp. 16, 23, 24; © Robert Barber, pp. 18, 30; © Jen & Des Bartlett/ Bruce Coleman, Inc., p. 21; © Wayne Lynch, p. 27; © Mary Ann McDonald/ CORBIS, p. 28; © Paul McCormick/ Image Bank/ Getty Images, p. 32; © Joe McDonald, p. 33. Cover: © age fotostock/ SuperStock.

Copyright © 2007 by Sandra Markle

Lerner Publications Company
A division of Lerner Publishing Group
241 First Avenue North
Minneapolis, MN 55401 U.S.A.

Website address: www.lernerbooks.com

Library of Congress Cataloging-in-Publication Data

Markle, Sandra.
  Skunks / by Sandra Markle.
    p.   cm. — (Animal prey)
  Includes bibliographical references and index.
  ISBN-13: 978−0−8225−6437−9 (lib. bdg. : alk. paper)
  ISBN-10: 0−8225−6437−8 (lib. bdg. : alk. paper)
  1. Skunks—Juvenile literature. I. Title. II. Series: Markle, Sandra.
  Animal prey.
  QL737.C248M37 2007
  599.76'8—dc22   2006000599

Manufactured in the United States of America
1 2 3 4 5 6 − DP − 12 11 10 09 08 07